2018 Miles

Nick O'Toole

BookLeaf Publishing

India | USA | UK

Presentation by *BookLeaf Publishing*

Web: www.bookleafpub.com

E-mail: info@bookleafpub.com

ISBN: 9789357448505

First edition 2022

DEDICATION

To my parents and grandparents, who got me here;

To all of the rats I've ever loved;

Above all, to Vicki, who encouraged my taking this poetry challenge and who inspires my writing every day that I'm alive.

ACKNOWLEDGEMENT

I'm writing this acknowledgement as I go, so it might be a bit all over the place.

I need to acknowledge my wonderful parents and grandparents, without whom I would not be here, who worked as hard as they did to give me every opportunity to even be able to write. There is no Me, and therefore no book, without Mum and Dad, without Pop or Nana, who raised, housed, and cared for me while I was growing up.

It's also vitally important that I acknowledge Mr Paul Stevens, one of my English teachers in High School. As well as being the coolest old guy I'd ever met, Mr Stevens was someone who thought I could write, and who went out of his way to encourage me to be better at it. I probably would have lost interest without him.

My friends have always been my primary audience for anything creative that I do, so obviously they get a shout out. Particularly Cameron, who was in all of my university writing classes and so has the technical skills to keep my writing strong. His feedback went a long way towards keeping these poems on track.

BookLeaf Publishing made this whole thing happen, it would be pretty dickish if I didn't thank them for the opportunity and the challenge to get this done. I'm a very lazy person until it becomes a challenge, so getting that fire started is definitely their doing.

Most importantly, my (at time of writing) fiancé Vicki. Since I met you, I have had a drive to grow as a person that just wasn't there before. If you weren't in my life, it would be a very different person wearing my face. You were the one who told me about this writing challenge, so this is your book too.
I can't wait to marry you.

PREFACE

There's never a thought that can't become a poem.

We tend to look at writers as extensions of their work, instead of the other way around. Poe isn't a writer, he's a GOTHIC writer. Attwood's not a writer, she's a FEMINIST writer. We study Henry Lawson for a term and by the end the most you'll say of him is "I guess he really loved the Outback". These are great writers, and they should be recognised, but I think it's a shame that they're mostly known for just one part of their personalities.

Poetry is one of the sincerest forms of thought that the written word can express. A collection of poetry, then, should give you a fair understanding of what a given poet thinks and feels about. In the age of influencers and bloggers, it's weird that poetry isn't thriving as a medium. It's even weirder that it still has this aura of inaccessibility, that it's only for specific people. We're in an age where every thought, every feeling can be made public for all the world to see, but we don't generally express them in verse? That's so weird.

This collection of 21 poems, written over 21 days, explores the way that "What do you think or feel?" is never as consistent as we might like it to be. We're always thinking, always feeling. In three short weeks, your mind can take you on a trip through more emotions and ideas than there are paths in the universe, and all of them deserve to be heard.

Inside this book, you'll find plenty of ideas; the struggle to self-motivate, the different things that bring us joy, the demons that visit in the night, and the entire range of feelings that go along with having loved ones. You'll find some that I think about a lot, and others that pass as wisps in the air, but all of them matter enough to reach the page.

They all matter enough to reach the page, because every thought, every dream, every idea that we ever have is part of what makes us who we are. We aren't just that time we thought about our parents, or the embodiment of our careers. We aren't even just vessels for love. We're all of those, but we're also the minutes between- the games that we play, the shows that we like, the endless thoughts upon thoughts we have every day- they all add up and make us human.

So these 21 poems, hopefully, will give you a
look at what made me up for 21 days- every idea
that crossed the mind.

There's never a thought that can't become a
poem.

The Lead Blimp -OR- Finding Motivation as a Severely Unmotivated Late-Twenties Millennial

The Lead Balloon is one of those elegant
metaphors:
how silly an idea, how poor a thing to think,
how much a waste of time, both mine and
yours?
Children know that a balloon should float,
we see the paradox, we know that lead will sink.
The image is so easy, the meaning so succinct,
It's simple, educational, it opens mental doors.

You know what isn't elegant? You know what
really sucks?
Having time, a writer's mind, a good idea and
more,
but never putting pen to page, 'cause
motivation's fucked.
The idea's that a lead balloon can never float.
Well floating's not enough, I need a stronger
metaphor,
It should fly at the very least, if not it should
soar.
Balloons have larger brothers, so good news,
we're all in luck.

The motivation problem is a massive, Leaden
Blimp.

It's easy just to have a really cool idea,
You hold it in your mental hands, turn it up and
down,
flip it over, shine it 'til it's nice and clear.
Visualising it's enough to make you float.
This crumb of an idea will be what turns your
life around,
It's gonna make you famous, gonna bring you
world-renown.
You smell it, taste it, it's a dream so very near!

The blimp just needs to get up in the air!

You've got the fire, set alight in your heart,
You have the gas, the thought's right there!
You're at the helm, it starts to float...

And then, like always, the fuel snap-freezes.
What you've built up stalls on the tarmac and
collapses.
(Do blimps even use tarmacs?)

Of course it fails, it's a blimp made of lead.
A bubble of motivation, now dead.
The words for the page are all trapped in your
head,
Your gift to the world, kept hidden instead.

Now unlike the balloon, always destined to fail,
the blimp isn't leaden all the way through.
You've seen it in flight, you've seen yourself
write,
You've ridden it before, driven it before;
Teachers swore that you'd achieve great things!

THIS BLIMP CAN FLY, DAMMIT!
IT'LL GET IN THE SKY, DAMMIT!
WE ARE GOING TO GAS IT UP,
AND WE ARE GOING TO WRITE,
DAMMIT!

Except now the blimp has gone unused.

Gears have rusted, wires have fused.
You've also lost the blueprints,
All you have is mental imprints,
which of course are all faded and pale,
hosed with miasma and stinking and stale,
you can't recall quite what the idea even looked
like at the start,
Or even get focused on where the idea is going
now.

So you put it back on the shelf, and maybe
you'll get to it later.
Which is of course when you notice the rest.
Every other Leaden Aircraft tucked away when
you lost the fire.

You could write, but it takes time
and besides that, it'll just be rejected.
You want to draw, well that'd be fine
If only you were feeling less dejected.
Losing weight? Well there's a goal!
Too bad you can't shift what you've collected.
Let's just be honest, overall,
The simple fact: you're disaffected.

This funk, this vile, empty stagnation
not only keeps you from your writing.
Weariness, and laziness, and fears
have chained up each of your ideas,

and every cause, each fight worth fighting.
So now, you're riled with indignation.

The blimp starts to fill up.
There's so much to write about,
there's so much reason to.

You want to write for writing's sake?
Well that's an air valve, but not a large one.
Why not write things you enjoy?
That valve's bigger, also more fun.
The lead blimp is filling up.

The blimp needs to be lighter than the air outside
it.
You know what makes your day light?
The thought of your loved ones is a handy
cliché,
but it gets you going, be that as it might.
The lead blimp is filling up.

You have thoughts, ideas and opinions
in massive amounts.
The world deserves to read them,
whatever, that counts.
THE LEAD BLIMP IS FILLING UP!

And then life offers you a challenge:
three simple words that start you flying:

"Bet you can't".

That's the spark.
The urge to prove them wrong-
The unkillable NEED to win-
The fools have made writing into a game!
AND NOW you're so FUCKING FULL
of BLUSTER and HOT AIR!

The leaden blimp is launched from off the floor,
And you're riding, driving it to Writing Town.
Your fingers o'er the keyboards glide and soar,
they're weightless now, you feel them float.
You'll write the best damn poetry around,
this blimp is never, EVER coming down!
I've time, a writer's mind, a good idea and more.

EPILOGUE
We're in the air, we're flying safe,
for now the blimp is stable.
The mania has passed
the radar is set to warn.
Life's lead can't stay gone forever,
we'll be grounded soon again.
But for now, we enjoy the ride
and hope it lasts.

Poetry Poem -OR- Evolving Thoughts on the Art Form From Age 14 to Now

I love metafiction, it's lovely to see.
So here's a poem about "poems and me":

INTRO / SONNET

My teaching came from people who
Enjoyed tradition in their words;
Where lines had beats and rhymes were 'true'
And "Free-Verse Crap" was never heard.

Now granted, they were very old,
Their heads were stuck inside the past,
"Ye'll take it from my death-grip cold!"
They always said until the last.

And I'll admit that at the time
I took their words inside my heart;
Assumed that knowing meter, rhyme,
Would make me master of the art.

The thing is, now I'm older too,
I have a more progressive view.

LET'S TALK ABOUT METER

I like TETRAMETER, myself.
I like the way the rhythm flows.
It's music written into words,
it lets them dance and makes them glow.

It has more of a songy feeling to it
than that of its more famous, older friend:
PENTAMETER, "the way the Shakespeares do
it".
With beats of five, and always rhyming end.
"Like human speech" is how we always knew it.

I will not touch HEXAMETER for very long.
So formal, self-important. Feels so off and
wrong.
It gives me awful deja-vu to time in school:

We learned about John Donne, the wretched
W;tless fool.
The man should really "Be Not Proud" of what
he's made.
He comes across so like a git who can't get laid.

Of course, there's always TRI,
precocious little guy.
How quick he flies on by.

FREE VERSE???

So now we've played around with meter,
and it was fun, if not restrained.
But standing clear, out from my peers
requires else than how I'm trained.
Free verse feels to me a lot like-
You dip your toes into a lake
but like-
the water is very thick?
And not in an unpleasant way
just like-
it's different.

You can splash around a bit,
And it still flows,
still moves in waves,
It still eddies out neatly.

And you could surely stay out here,
Floating free from the usual steady rock
but to stay too long would be to forget,
to stay too long would be to abandon.

RHYME

Free verse tends to quietly smother
the link twixt me and secret lover,
the love affair I can not cover:
I need my Rhyme like none-another.

Mother Rhyme, most delightful, musical
Lover who typically comes last, so for
another small experiment we'll try to
cover the start of a line with rhyme instead.

Mmmmmm nope, that feels weird.

Why not design a sublimely fine, poetic line that
confines nine rhymes at a time? How divine!

Well, aside from the rebel thrills,
to do it strains your vocab skills,
and showing off like that just kills
any further interest to read.
Also the "M/N" dissonance
is closer then to Assonance

Than the constant consonants
that truly 'true rhyme' needs.

OUTRO/ SONNET

I bullied Hexameter being so formal,
rejected Pentameter's closeness to 'normal',
My poetry journey has taken some turns
and now years later, some things that I've
learned:

Traditional formats I deeply respect,
but don't think they need us to fiercely protect.
Rigidity's nice and I still love to rhyme,
but free verse is fun too- some of the time.

Sorry to those from conservative schools,
Poetry can't be constricted by rules.
The format is for letting feelings run free,
So being strict on it don't sit right with me.

I planned to end off with a proper sonnet,
but this isn't a rhyming couplet.
And now it isn't fourteen lines either.

I'm Getting Married -OR- I Really Hope we Aren't Delayed Again, Gimme the Ring!

I know we had to change the date,
I know we've waited for two years,
but still I know it's worth the wait,
our special day is coming near.

I know that you remember,
better, probably, than me,
how this all started.
How you and I started talking,
how we met on a foundation
that most would look at and say
"I'd never build a house on that!"

Because let's face it,
a tinder is for starting fires
and fires tend to self-extinguish,
OR catastrophically consume everything
and then die anyway.

On top of that,
it's not like I had the best fuel.
"Guinea Pig Mummy?"
It was confusion and very uncharming.
But where I'd bought my fuel at like,
Crazy Clark's Discount Warehouse,
at least it was better than stealing it
from a back-alley dealer
like Mister "Tongue-Punch".

But, I guess some effort is better than none
and clearly you thought so too.
Because we got it off the ground.

It isn't like we're new to waiting.
We 'dated' for a bit before it
officially was labelled dating,
and now I think we're stronger for it.

I can't believe you got me travelling.
I hate travelling.
But somehow going with you-
It's like hating peanuts forever,
and then one day you have a Snickers,
and suddenly it's like
"Oh hey, peanuts don't suck".

I've been to Brisbane maybe three times
but because two of those were with you
there's this solid map,
burned in my brain,
entangled with holding your hand there
and now that city is just
burned in my brain,
because you took me there.

The houses I grew up in?
I don't even recall them.
But I can picture in vivid detail
the wonderful BnB in Grafton
because you were so happy there.
And because I knew then.
You'd taken a road trip to Grafton,
with me,
so that I could play a day of cards.
You didn't need to be there
But you came and supported me
and I knew then.

Another thing you waited for:
to pop the question and the ring.
I my defence, I wasn't sure
of how to do the perfect thing.

Another thing you gave me,
or rather, I gave you
was opening my heart
to our first pets together.

I'd had pets before,
as a kid.
It was not the same.
They were family pets,
I never had to look after them,
not really.
This was very different.

By circumstantial fortune,
you were away during that week
leading up to your birthday.
I'd known for months what I was getting you.
You grew up with guinea pigs
"Guinea Pig Mummy"

and I thought rats might be better
as we didn't have an outside.
I got the cage, and on the day you were coming
home
I bought the rats.
The first two.

The look on you when you saw them!
I'd made you come through the door eyes
closed.
You gasped, in the loveliest way,
and stood there in shock.
I saw you love them,
so I loved them too,
and that was the difference.
They weren't just a pet,
they were yours, ours.
A living connection between us.

I imagine that's what kids might be like.
I certainly hope so,
if we come to it.
It's a scary, enthralling idea.

But at this point,
come what may,
I know at least one thing:
My life with you belongs to us,
belongs to every emotion,

every memory we've made.
The people from before we met,
don't really exist now.
The wedding certificate is really
a birth certificate
for what we've made each other.

It's been two years we've been engaged,
I asked you then to be my wife.
And I can't wait to turn the page,
to read about our wedded life.

Pet Rats -OR- One of Those Conversations I Somehow Have Too Damn Often

It's common to have cats or dogs as your pet,
but here's one you might not have thought about
yet.

Sit yourself down, it's time that we chat,
about what life's like when you own a rat.
No, firstly, hey, get that look off your face.
Rat owners see it all over the place.
That look of revulsion, the look of disgust,
the eyes all'a'sudden turned dark with mistrust.
It makes us all hurt, it makes us all sad,
you need to be told why your thinking is bad.
It's clear that this talk is of utmost import,
it's obvious this fight just has to be fought.

Now let's start it easy, without being vague:
No, rats can't give you a bit of the plague.
Leaving aside that you'd likely live through it,
human-owned ratties just simply won't do it.
"Heh, surely not, do you think I'm a fool?
We all learned of gross, nasty rats in our
school".
My friend, aside from that terrible slander,
it sounds like you've gobbled some gross
propaganda.
You might get infected by flea or by tick,
but those kinds of bites'll make anyone sick.
You know what has those? Your dog and your
cat.
OH NO! I bet you weren't thinking 'bout that?

The next thing they say, just to make us all hurty,
"Are rats on the whole not notoriously dirty?"
I challenge you simply to watch, you will see.
A ratty will clean himself better than me.
They clean themselves literally all of the time,
They don't abide filth and they don't abide
grime.
They clean because frankly (going back to
diseases),
pretty much everything gives them the sneezes.
The poor little buggers can't risk getting sick.
A body that small gets real bad pretty quick.
I will say their odor can get a bit strong,

but regular cleaning their cage can't go wrong.

There is though one point I'll give over to you:
the small toothy bastards like having a chew.
They're rodents, so although they're
ever-so-little,
Their teethies are always in need of a whittle,
and I thought for sure that they'd all go for
wood-
but nope, no, nuh-uh, that just isn't as good.
You know what they want? To chew on your
sheets.
Your clothes and your towels will make for good
eats.
Oh, and they'll eye you off, all the while
grinnin'
stuffing their faces all full of your linen.
I've spent so much on cheapies at K-Mart.
But after all that, let's get to the good part.

Firstly they're smart, exceedingly clever.
I'll never get past that part of them ever.
Give one a puzzle, he'll figure it out,
Especially if he knows treats are about.
They memorise faces, never forget you,
In a full room it's you who they'll get to.
They love to learn, they're easily trained,
(and that's how that they're so clean is
explained).

Rats are all full, just loaded, with poos.
All through the day they store up number twos.
But give them a week with one box of litter,
and they'll only use that one box as a shitter.

Intelligent creatures will all love to play,
And rats are no different, they'll do it all day.
They love to play tag, they'll play
hide-and-seek,
they'll do it with style, and smiles, and cheek.
They love a good climb, they love to explore,
so be sure you keep a good watch on the door.
Remember you're big, and he's very small.
He'll wait patiently for your defense to fall.
If one gets away, he'll find a good place
to sit snug and smug as he laughs at your face.
He knows you're to big to reach him in here!
Remember, he's playing, it's all in good cheer.

And finally, listen, 'cos here's the best part:
ratties are just balls of hair with big hearts.
The love of a rat can't be overstated,
Nor should their empathy be underrated.
As much as your rat will enjoy getting fun in,
if you're in the dumps he's the first one to run
in.
Amazing how something so small can perceive
it,
But I've seen first-hand, so I can believe it.

as much as a dog might be able to tell,
if you're sad a ratty will feel it as well.
He loves you so much, so if you're feeling down
He'll cuddle on up until life turns around.

They're beautiful animals, I'll never regret
bringing them home to love as my pet.
The one, single flaw, I'm sad to report:
their sweet, little lives are painfully short.
They'll come to your life, they'll learn to do
puzzles,
they'll play, they'll poop, they'll give you their
nuzzles,
and after it all, when it all comes to end,
You'll get to cherish the life of your friend.
You'll have their love from moment of meeting,
and it will be precious because it's so fleeting.

So, with all of that said, you'd best not forget
there's naught a bad thing 'bout a rat as your pet.

Nightmare 1 -OR- Work for Work's Sake Scares Me

Unsure of how,
unsure of why,
I am only sure that I have died.
I have died and this is my afterlife.
I did not expect there to be an afterlife.

A desk, cubicle walls, stale air above
Somehow all the most sterilised white,
Somehow all sickly artificial,
Somehow more piercingly bright,
than the computer screen in front of me,
and Somehow more attractive to the eye.

This office(?) is devoid of sound
and yet every minute detail hums,
every corner drones,
with the expectation,
with anticipation,
with sheer DEMAND that I perform my role.

A role I am unsure of.

It's clear that I should be working.
That's what I was hired for.
That's why I'm here.
That's how I arrived in this too-bright cell,
at this computer that is boring to look at,
with the drone that is boring into my skull.

There is no way to mark how long I've been
here.
There is a clock, of course, ticking away.
But it doesn't tell me how long I've been here.
Somehow it only tells me
how much company time I've been wasting
here.
I've been wasting here.

It's important that I don't waste their time
I can't let myself waste their time.
The company's time must be spent productively.
You were given a job to take up your time.
Your time is marked, they pay by the hour.
By wasting time, you're robbing the company.

If only I could remember the job.
There are other workers, there must be.

Why would there be cubicles if not to separate
the workers?
Asking one of them what to do would surely
help.
Sure, and then the bosses would know.
They'd know that you couldn't keep a simple
task in mind.
Unlike the others, soundlessly clacking at their
keyboards.

The back of my head is screaming,
the connection between skull and spine,
is shouting, crying, bawling,
because it knows we'll be fired.
We can't do the simple task we were assigned
and it means we'll be fired.

No job means no work
no work means no money
no money means no food
no food means no living-

A redder, thicker part of the brain interrupts.
Being stuck here, hours upon years,
is that truly living?
Are we living?
I thought we had died.
What use then is there in the work?

The logic is sound,
but it is only one sound
alone amongst the droning.
The computer's droning,
the endless, brain-boring,
mind numbing
droning.

And so the lone sound,
with the sound logic
is droned out,
silenced by that knowledge,
the certainty,
that THEY will check on my work soon.

The nameless, faceless THEY,
Breathing down necks,
breathing on the connection between skull and
spine,
fanning the frozen flames of fear.

Just do SOMETHING,
I try to tell my hands.
Anything to try to satiate,
anything that might pass off,
anything to be productive,
and suddenly my hands are flying
across the keyboard, adding thunderous cracks
to the droning silence of the cubicle.

But though I type for what must be an eternity,
somehow there is nothing on the screen.
Just an endless square of light,
the edges becoming tendrils,
grasping at my eyes,
fondling my sight,
keeping my focus locked in.
"Look at what you have done,
See how you deserve this,
Understand that this nothingness is yours".

I break its hold to see the clock
the clock that somehow has not moved.
Or maybe
Maybe the clock has cycled completely through
again.
Somewhere between timelessness
and eternity.
This nothingness is mine.

And now the droning has become a voice
demanding my results,
needing my completed tasks,
screeching for my efforts,
and when I try to defend myself
I find that I have no voice
no power here, no mouth.

I have no mouth, and I must protest
But I can't.

I am removed.
gently, softly, I am removed.
Violently ripped from my station.
thrown to the ether.
They were not happy.
No job means no work
no work means no money
no money means no food
no food means no living-

But this is better.
I was not living anyway.
Amid everything, this is a glimmer
a baseline of hope.
To become nothing would at least
break from the monotony.
A shimmer of light.

A shimmer of pure light
Suddenly and immediately contrasted
with the artificial light
of my newest laptop and cubicle.

Somewhere between timelessness
and eternity.
A desk, cubicle walls, stale air above

Somehow all the most sterilised white,
Somehow all sickly artificial,
Somehow more piercingly bright,
I have no task, and I must work.

Stuck Inside -OR- I Swore I Wasn't Going to Date Myself With a COVID Poem, but Here We Are

You know how sometimes you can see a cat,
and it'll spend the whole damn day asleep?
It's lying there, it's snoozing, getting fat,
and if you try to wake it, not a peep?

But when you lock the cat up for the night,
it's suddenly a super active cat,
who will not stay inside without a fight?
For me the lockdown's quite a bit like that.

I like the great indoors, sequestered from the
sun.
I find that things outside are really not as fun.

Inside I get to read, inside are games to play.
Inside is films and things I get to do throughout
the day.

Outside are bees and spiders, outside are funny
smells,
Outside the weather's either cold or hot as hell.
And living in Australia, a short walk from the
sun,
is any wonder why the outdoors make me run?

But here's the thing my guy.
we're at a point where I
am tired of inside.
Am tired of staying put.
Am over watching films.
Am sick of being stuck.

I hear their voice online,
and maybe that'd be fine,
but somehow it defines
the isolation's grip,
the way that yin and yang
are both a coin to flip.

I miss faces.
I miss you.
I miss my friends.
I want to get together and play.

I want to stretch my legs.
I even miss going to work,
because I miss having something to do
not-at-home.

And here's the thing, I get it, by the way:
The public health has got to come in first.
I understand that we all have to stay,
or else the fucking virus will get worse.

But maybe, maybe, maybe hear me out:
This fucking thing might not have been so long,
if certain people hadn't fucked about,
and gotten such a simple thing so wrong.

Well hey now, sure, we should of-course be fair:
for who alive of millions would've seen
the people going after Medicare
would fuck the country's rollout of vaccines?

And who would fucking think
that getting on the drink
would be such a priority
above our health security?
The "demon in a bottle"
feels so appropriate,
because what else would possess you,
what arrogance infects you,
to fuck an entire country

for one fucking party?

And now that we have a solution,
now that we have a vaccine,
I can't even grasp the notion
that you would dare refuse it
because somehow it became political.
Get over yourself.

I DON'T EVEN LIKE GOING OUTSIDE!
But being unable?
I'm so angry,
I'm so tired,
I'm so over being stuck
being punished
for some other dipshit's mistake.

Most of all:
I'm tired of being tired.
I'm angry at myself for being angry.
I miss not missing people.
I want to not be wanting.
Knowing that it will end
does not make it better now.

Time to Duel -OR- Personal Reflection on a Life-Long Obsession with Card Games

I really love card games.

It's just you at a table, and someone across,
Between you a fully flat warzone.
In one hand, your deck, your cards.
In the other, anticipation for the game.
The minute before it starts,
introductions, a chat, a sporting handshake,
Shuffle and cut, "Roll for first?"
Play is decided, hands are drawn
And Player One takes their turn.

A long time ago, I was but a wee lad,

absorbed by the colours and light of the telly,
I watched a cartoon, one that I never had,
and watching it struck up a fire in my belly.

All that I understood, crushed into shards,
reshuffling everything I'd ever been
A show from Japan about fighting with cards.
Was unlike anything I'd ever seen.

If pressed on why it struck, I'd guess to tell:
alone of all the other shows I saw,
a kid like me could play these games as well;
So now I had a goal worth aiming for.

That game wasn't long.
They were playing something rogue-
A deck outside of what you'd expect
at least, for competitive play.
It was weird anyway
and you're here to win,
so you do.
Because of course you're playing something
good.
There's a twenty-dollar promo to win.
The next round is called to play.

"Oh Mother, Mummy, oh my Mum most dear,
oh please would you just buy for me these
cards?
You know that I've done well at school this year,
you know that I've been working oh so hard."

So she gives in and gives me that first pack,
it starts it all, the very sweetest taste.
I'm lost forever now and won't come back;
The gods have sent a gift and I've been graced.

The pack falls open like it's barely there.
I hold the cards and can't do more than laugh.
I'm dancing now without a single care,
there's no way off this gilded cardboard path.

Three rounds over now.
Three wins, about what you'd thought.
It could just be good luck,
That so far you've had it easy.
That rounds four and five will come
and you'll be hit by actual good players.
OR it could just be
that you're the best there is,
and the wins are all deserved.

I want to play the cards seen in the show:
the wizards, dragons, all of them so cool.
And since I care more than the kids I know,
it's quite enough to beat the kids at school.

Until, of course, I get past primary,
and all my peers are suddenly smarter,
My style of play's in need of refinery,
I need to learn to play a bit harder.

It takes a while to build back up my skill
to match against the smarter, older kids.
I set a goal to overcome that hill,
and after growing, learning hard, I did.

Round Four was not quite a disaster
but you were pushed.
You had to fight for it,
And well you should,
you played against your friend.
You know that they're very good
But of course, in your heart
You know that you're just better
and into Round 5, you hold it.

With adulthood you start to realise, yuck,
I have to pay for cards and things myself.
With bills, a job, and all the other muck,
my cards spend more and more time on the
shelf.

But that obsession never waits for long,
and as I've gotten old the game has too,
it's that progression, keeps it going strong;
the game is more than something else to do.

For decades now, I've had the memories,
the good, the bad, the competition days,
amazing friends, and even enemies
united by the silly game we play.

The last round is over.
The table's a mess.
Cards are in messy piles.
Reality's back in place now
You shake their hand.
You get back over it:
The loss, and your own ego.
You did not win the twenty.
But you had a great time doing it.

The Hunter -OR- Ballad of a Video Game I Really Like

Gather 'round, ye children
and let me set the scene:
The story of the greatest Hunter
there has ever been.
A bird and human hybrid,
bedecked in red and gold,
a laser cannon on her arm,
a Hunter brave and bold.

Way back on Planet Zebes,
her home of K-2L
was ransacked by some Pirates
and was blown to living hell.

Well in the long years after,
the Hunter trained and grew.
Until one day the Federation's
mission came on through.

The Hunter's Zero Mission:
return and infiltrate
the colony of Pirates and
send them to meet their fate.

The Hunter flew, a quick return
alone, against all odds.
She plumbed its depths and blasted down
the Pirates and their gods.

Til finally the Hunter found
the weapon she had sought:
the Life-Form Known as Metroid.
And she blew it all to nought.

Her Zero-Mission ended,
The Hunter rose to fame.
The Federation gave her thanks
and lionised her name.
The creatures she had found though,
those gave them all a scare.
She had to make sure there could not
be more Metroids out there.

The Hunter's Prime is legend,
in Echoes it is told,
but stories get Corrupted so
they shakily unfold.
A power known as Phazon grew

and swallowed many worlds
The Hunter saved the galaxy!
or so the tale's unfurled.

The Metroids had a homeworld,
Known as SR388.
The Hunter chooses to Return
and then exterminate.

An artificial living thing,
the Metroid was created,
with hunger for life energy
that went unsatiated.

She has a pretty simple plan,
By now, the trick is old.
Of course she gets a shock to learn,
The Metroids have evolved.

So deep within the Chozo labs,
where nothing's left alive
The Hunter takes out everything
within the Metroid hive.

With no more Metroids living,
she finds a single egg.
It hatches and through mercy,
she lets it live instead.

She takes the hatchling Metroid,
a docile one, at least.
It's studied in captivity,
the Galaxy's at peace.
Alas the peace is fragile,
The Hunter's in for more.
The Baby's cute, but it can't know
the danger that's in store.

The Pirates, feeling vengeful,
in fierce retaliation,
attacked and stole the Baby from
the Ceres Research Station.

Alight with rage, the Hunter chased.
To Zebes they returned.
She vowed to give the Pirates all
the vengeance they had earned.

The Pirates had rebuilt their base,
Resumed their vile plan
To clone and use the Metroids so
to pilfer every land.

Of course the Pirates weren't too smart.
they overfed their prize,
The Baby couldn't be controlled
When it grew to Super-size.

The Hunter made it through the world,
she beat them once again.
And with the Metroid's sacrifice
she took out Mother Brain.

She'd wiped out all the Metroids,
each and every one,
but all she had was melancholy
for the job she'd done.
Still the stories of her deeds
had made her name so great,
the Federation brought her back
to SR388

It was a simple mission,
It should have been so light.
Instead the Hunter was attacked
by cruel X- Parasites.

The X would eat you inside-out
and steal your DNA,
your knowledge and your powers,
all while you'd melt away.

If they were left to go unchecked,
the world would all be dead.
And so, so they could eat the X,
the Metroids had been bred.

The Hunter was infected now,
and worse she'd never been,
until from Metroid DNA
they crafted a vaccine.

She made it through, a Fusion,
her life owed to the Baby.
The Hunter took a final job,
"Any objections, Lady?"

'Twas many moons ago indeed,
passed since that fateful date.
The only thing we know is that
there's no more 388.
The Hunter's passed to mystery,
for years she's gone unseen,
with no recorded history
to speak of where she's been.

There's rumours that the Pirates though
all Dread of her return.
To see The Hunter come again-
is something that I yearn.
Gather 'round, ye children,
the scene is now well-set:
The story of the greatest Hunter
hasn't ended yet.

Wine -OR- This Used to Hurt Less Ten Years Ago

Your clock goes off at six,
Or rather, I assume.
You're off to work and quick,
you leave me in the room.

And well and good.
It's Sunday-
just the beep-beep-beep
throbs inside my head,
a dancing nightclub beat,
plays and bounces 'round
within the sea of red
sloshing around my guts and grey matter-
an organic goblet for pre-drunk wine.

I spend an hour in trying,
in battling the dead.
I need to stop the lying,
I need to clear my head.

And well and good.
To waste the day?
It simply shouldn't do.
There's eight toll-free hours left.
Still blurry, grumbling, tumbling,
Rediscovering the too-familiar path.
Making my fumbling way
to the ever-holy throne
to flush the system out.

The morning hang is gone,
and so like last weekend,
I say it won't go on,
I promise "not again".

It's an easy promise, really.
On Sunday
The morning after a good night,
Doing the Lord's work by not working.
Then I get the rest of the week.
Doing some actual work, by working.
and that very final hour before the Friday bell-
The one that goes for infinity-
The Bottle-O is so close to home…

It's Saturday tonight,
I'll have a little drink,
"a little bit's alright",

I tell myself, I think.

A little bit is all I have, truly.
Some dressing with dinner, frankly.
A smidge, while I watch my weekend show.
Another episode, another drop won't hurt.
Another drop. Oh go on.
Another episode? Why not?
I have nowhere to be tomorrow.
That bottle's only a glass-full.
Can't let it be lonely now.

Your clock goes off at six;
I dread the coming doom.
You're up, you're out and quick,
you leave me in the room.

The List -OR- Ten Things I Love About You

However do I love thee?
Let me count the ways-
The thoughts that cross upon my heart
when you are in my gaze.

Up first among your attributes:
I love the way you're strong,
That your infectious strength can help
us all to carry on.
The way you can't be pushed around,
the way you won't be wronged.
When people try, they never get
away with it for long.

I love your sense of humour, though
I think it learned from mine.
I love they way our jokes can match,
the way they make you shine.
And like with mine they can't all land
but when they do they're fine.

If we could joke forever, then
we'd have a life divine.

I love the way you've got so much
tucked up inside your brain;
that I can come with questions when
a problem is a pain.
You've got a clear solution for
a lot of mental drain,
and let me benefit from all
the knowledge you have gained.

And one that might surprise you is:
I love your music taste.
You're right to think it's not for me,
my ears have not been graced.
If I believed I'd like it, then
the faith would be misplaced.
But I cannot deny the light
it brings upon your face.

And since we're on the topic here:
The fiction you enjoy.
It's quirky and it's different
from when I was a boy.
I know I like to bully it,
but that's just being coy;
'cos even when it isn't great,
it's something you enjoy.

I also love how you do hobbies,
the ways you go all in.
And even though compared to mine,
your hobby time is thin,
a finished project gets from you
a cute, triumphant grin.
I love the drive you have inside
that pushes you to win.

On this you'll disagree with me:
I love the way you look.
The way you are in each and all
the photographs we took.
It's even when you're at your worst,
it's even when you're crook.
I said you'd disagree but you're
not reading from my book.

I love the things I do not love,
of which there are a few.
They might annoy me slightly, but
they're still a part of you.
I'll take them all, if I did not,
it wouldn't be as true.
I love all of the greatest parts,
The not-so great ones too.

For number nine, I think I'll say,

The way you love and care.
How when you've got a thing to love,
the love you always share.
And sometimes when it's all for me,
the love in you is bare.
You've got a look when you're in love,
I love to see it there.

Which brings us then to number ten:
I love the love I feel.
When things are broken, just the thought
of you can make it heal,
You put the feelings in my heart,
which makes it yours to steal.
The feelings you inspire in me;
like nothing else is real.

I love so much that I love you,
and how much you love me.
We're getting hitched and I can't think
of better ways to be.

I Am Rat -OR- An Account of a Day in the Very Hard Life of a Pet Rat

I want to have a chat,
so let me tell you that
it's sweet to be a rat.
The days begin all covered-
or rather I'd say smothered-
up by your loving brothers.

The first one up is Mum,
and to the cage she comes
to scritch me on my bum.
Then off she goes away,
she does it every day,
to earn a bit of pay.

I guess I'll have a pee,
Then back to sleep for me.
It's still too dark to see.
I curl up in the puddle,

the little ratty huddle.
We all enjoy a cuddle.

And that's when Dad awakes,
comes over here and takes
us up as morning breaks.
He puts us on the bed,
he pats us on the head,
and shares a bit of bread.

He lets us run around,
but really starts to frown
if we head for the ground.
But if I could get under
the bed I'd have to wonder
what goods there are to plunder.

He picks us up and then
we're in the cage again,
myself and all my friends,
and Dad says that it's late,
"it's almost half past eight".
He calls us "Sweet Potates"

And then he goes as well,
as far as I can tell.
It's quiet now as hell-
Until I get a fright,
I'm jumped on from the right,

my brother wants to fight.

Don't worry, it's all fun.
We biff a bit, we run,
it's simply how it's done.
We rats, we like to rumble,
a bicker and a tumble.
Not graceful, more a bumble.

That's pretty much the way
we get to spend our day.
It's pretty good I'd say.
The eating when we choose,
retiring then to snooze,
and sometimes doin' poos.

Then after time has passed,
our Mum is home at last.
We jump to see her, fast!
We play some ratty games,
she calls us silly names.
We love her all the sames.

When Dad gets home as well, he
will scritch us on our belly
and then he'll call us smelly,
which I don't know the meaning,
but from a guess I'm gleaning,
it's good because he's beaming.

They scoop up me, my friends;
we're in the cage and then
we'll do it all again,
when night becomes the morning,
when day again is dawning,
I think about it, yawning.

So first I'll have a pee,
Then off to sleep for me.
a rat is good to be.
I curl up in the puddle,
the little ratty huddle.
We all enjoy a cuddle.

Tiger and House-Cat -OR- I'm Not Always Sure Which One of These I Am

House-Cat and Tiger met
one night in Bast's Plains,
a dream shared amongst the world's cats
as a group.

The Tiger, feline king
had seen many cats
all passing through this sacred place,
young and old.

The House-Cat, daisy fresh,
first time on the Plains,
Just barely past its kittenhood
excited.

Kind Tiger understood.
To House-Cat, "Welcome!
You've reached our great ancestral plane!
How do you?"

House-Cat knows not Tiger.
He knows only that
Here's where he can make his first mark
and be known.

Said House-Cat to Tiger,
"Let me(ow) show you-
a trick most important and base-
how to hunt".

Proud Tiger, old as time,
amusedly grins-
With aim to mollify House-Cat-
"Oh please, do".

House-Cat doesn't know yet;
Bast always provides,
that hunting here has no purpose.
Our secret.

Tiger knows, but silently.
Won't ruin the fun.
House-Cat wants to hunt, so appears
Mouse, small, cute.

House-Cat crouches, spies Mouse,
dusts the air, swish, swish-
A plane at port prepared to launch-
he misses.

Tiger, aside, giggles.
"Ah indeed! Good show-
like a skunk crafting sweet perfumes-
informative!"

House-Cat ends his lesson,
"And now, like me(ow)-
Tiger knows how to find his lunch-
Have fun friend!"

Tiger turns and gets down low,
chuckling still again-
"perhaps were I a cub, maybe"-
Tiger stalks.

Tiger is a reverse flame,
consumed by the grass-
an elephant hidden by shrubs-
Tiger hunts.

No swish, swish from Tiger.
Just silent burning-
the grass, the ground, the air and then-
Tiger eats.

Fathers -OR- With Deepest Respect and Apologies to Ian Mudie

Some peoples' fathers begin as Gods,
arbiters and omniscient, divinely powerful,
untoppled by all until they decide otherwise,
setters of commandments and punishers of
broken rule.
Through age, those fathers are brought mortal;
the growing child questions their faith,
and without prayer the God becomes Man-
regular and routine and rote.
Then as the child becomes Man,
as they reach the same level,
some faith might be restored
and experience forges connection.
Never again do either reach Godhood,
except to their own children,
turning the wheel of divinity again.

Other fathers begin as Superheroes.

They're Supermen, strong, smart,
fantastically, unrealistically cool.
Worth looking up to. Worth admiring.
Creating a façade, a legend,
a projection on a glass frame,
ready to be shattered by the smallest pebble.
The child sees the alter-ego,
and not every Man of Steel
is Clark Kent at home.
Superheroism becomes then a full-time job,
and best not dare to slip up-
worse still, slip to the dark side.
A villainous descent hurts more
from such a high peak.

Superheroes or Gods, they are lionised.
Godhood is granted by naive eyes,
eyes searching for answers
in a new and scary world.
Godhood then is taken away
once the eyes start to see.
Superheroism is granted through deeds,
a constant state of goodness,
one that it is unhuman to maintain.
'Superheroism' is not a default state.
Not a stamp you get for breeding.
Superheroism is purposeful.
Breeding happens by accident daily.
Superhero or God, these labels are picked up-

assumed as part of the package,
often even demanded, without being earned.
Love is not a default setting.

All that said:
This wasn't even a blip to me, never even
occurred,
until I started to meet other people-
Other people, with their other dads.
Other people, with their other dads,
Creating a void against which mine
May as well be the sun.

My father did not begin as a God.
My father did not begin as a Superhero.
My father did not even begin as a Dad.
I had already begun when he joined us.
And he joined us as a man.
A man with human thoughts and feelings,
A man who, not being a God, was actually there.
A man who, not being a Superhero, could be
real.
A man with a heart.

A lion will eat the cubs that threaten his Pride.
Lions are not alone in that.
My dad was never so simple as a lion.
My dad found my family,
He made it his own family,

and as he would with many homes,
he strengthened it, expanded it,
he made it better than before.

Because he was not a God,
he did not click his fingers and make it happen.
Because he was not a Superhero,
he did not assume perfection from the start.
Because he was just a man,
he did it with his own hands,
through the strength he had as a man.
Because he was just a man,
I learned how to be one too.

My father did not begin as a God, or a
Superhero.
Superheroes are a romantic, unrealistic ideal.
For me to say he was divine would be an insult.
All his life, my dad has only ever been a man.
A great man, who rather than a God or
Superhero
chose to be a dad.
Chose to be my dad.
Because he was just a man,
I know how I want to be too.

Mum -OR- I Couldn't Be Here Without You

When did you become my mum?
Well that's a pretty easy one.
You've been her from the very start,
you've always played the special part.
I can't remember it so well.
I'd just been born, but people tell:
The people who I've asked all say
you've been one since the starting day.
And I don't see the evidence
to offer any difference,
so knowing what I know of you,
so trusting that the story's true:
You've always been my mum.

But what point did I realise?
At what point did I recognise?
How good a mum you'd always been,
of all the mums there've ever been.
A lot of mums have often stressed
that for their kids they want the best,

and something that I know of you
is just how much that statement's true,
the love and the encouragement
you've put to our development,
the things you've given on this track
and how you'd never take it back-
At some point, I realised.

So when did you become my friend?
With whom I just like time to spend?
A person who I'd call by choice,
because I like to hear your voice?
To ask about the things you've seen,
to ask you how your day has been-
To hear about your life's report,
and shoot the shit and share a thought.
And I don't have to search to see,
it's not a commonality.
It's strange to really think about,
but it's true, I've got no doubt.
At some point you became my friend.

And you've become my hero too.
I'll try so much to be like you.
You've been a person to admire,
a standard I want to aspire,
to live up to your shining soul,
along the way became a goal.
I hope my own kids get to see

that part of you reflect in me.
To give as much, to be as kind,
a better mum you'd never find.
By being you, in being Mum,
you make me proud to be your son.

Thank you.

Nightmare 2 -OR- Recurring Dream of Being Trapped in a Familiar-Yet-Strange Home

We two approached it,
the "house".
More accurately:
the Domicile.

Sulfuresque in colour and texture,
like making your eyes bite into a rotten egg.
The first bite releases the smell
and it fills your lungs and you wonder,
"Why are we here again?"

Memory clicks over,
the squishy pink brick
rolls;
on the underside,

a barely registered scrawl,
chicken scratch carved with a rusted chain:
"to con him"

Who is "him"?
Blank.
Why must he be conned?
Blank
Is there a reason for it all to be
Blank?

We knock, the two of us.
The door opens,
a hot and sour breath exits,
like laying down in front of a sleeping dog.
I even swear that there is slime,
drooling from the upper lip-
though I guess it could just be mould.

The person-
the individual-
the being, inside-
seems shapeless.
a face, not necessarily a head,
atop a blobby mess
wrapped in denim.

Denim that is too blue,
vibrant and not faded,
neon that distracts from all,

From the pockmarked face above,
from the globules of flesh it covers,
from the clay-red décor of the room,
complete with… orange? stains.

The eternal and momentary shock of it all
reminds me of my-
sorry, "our"-
our purpose.
Insurance.
"Would you like some insurance, sir?"

We are invited to the kitchen,
and as we squelch there it occurs,
how strange it is
to have made it through the door,
let alone,
deeper into the Domicile,
when normally our only stop is the step.
And how strange it is,
that we "squelch" through a home;
it's… not a normal sound?

The colours and stains
have deepened,

red-to-brown now,
and those are definitely orange.
Also!- no…
surely walls don't usually ooze?

We've reached the kitchen-
I assume anyway-
it has a sink,
an esky leaking water.
I would have asked,
would have enquired,
but there was nobody to ask.

Suddenly just myself,
staring up at me from
the puddle from the esky.
Grotesquely Picassoan me,
Myself and I,
and an empty room
of orange and brown.

I could swear I had been led here?
Walked behind a man
and beside a partner? But
the Domicile assures me,
its chasmous emptiness as proof,
I must be faulty.

Alone, knowing this isn't my home,
it's time to dig my way out.

Darkening maroon and sparking orange,
a wall where I was sure there was a walkway,
laughed at me,
or coughed,
or spluttered?
some uncomfortable noise spewing forth,
out of seemingly fresh stains.

Stains that smile,
only the smile is a snarl,
a cheekless grin,
teeth-stains,
like a bite of overripe strawberries
without the actual fruit.
just the stains and the bite.

And then a call,
a shout from a freshly revealed doorway,
complete with the assurance
that this is my new way out.

I was here to sell something.
cookies?
A product of some kind.

The Domicile turns

and twists,
it bends:
a vile intestine,
complete with the stench
of yesterday's digested breakfast.

I, no longer "we"
(like I'm sure I was at the start),
follow the path of red and orange.
Hoping that,
like the breakfast,
I'll find the back door,
if not the front.
and finally,

Memory recalls,
a hieroglyph in the squishy pink brick,
the Domicile's owner.
The fleshy body with the pockmarked face.

But memory also recalls
incredibly colourful clothes,
which have seemingly been replaced
with the friend I walked in with.

Two bodies, twisted-
twisting?-

together.
a mound eating itself,
or possibly rutting about
in a Lovecraftian facsimile
of love-making.

A face, one or the other,
or possibly both at once,
emerges from the mass.
Noise issues forth,
possibly a question,
probably a threat.

I don't remember leaving
the Domicile.
I only recall those colours-
I think-
but even they fade.

We two approached it,
the house,
to sell our raffle tickets.
$2:50 to work the cause.

Teacher Thoughts -OR- An Anthology of Loose Thoughts About the Job

I am an English teacher, and
I teach some Maths as well.
So here's a bunch of smaller thoughts
I think I'd like to tell.

To teach The Bard is loads of fun,
I really get some massive kicks
from pointing out how rude he is,
and how his plays are full of dicks.

I've taught a lot of kids by now,
and all of them learn differently.
And though they all have different strengths,

I'll say with perfect certainty:

No single kid knows how fractions work.

My heart agrees, and says you're right,
You probably don't need
to be in Senior English if
you're never gonna read.

And if I had the power, then,
I think I'd leave you be
But sad for you, I must obey
the nasty DET.

It's fine if you don't want to read,
but let me make it clear:
if you don't pick that book up soon
You're gonna fail the year.

The thing is, yes you're funny.
You're good at getting laughs.
But now is not the time or place,
please see me after class.

We're told that kids are precious,
by those who've managed to forget
that some kids are kinda vicious,
and all are smarter than you'd bet.

How greatly do I wish
that I could also see that wall
and find myself lost
in whatever fantastic void
you seem to have found.

Sure, you're here to learn,
But my pets did something cute!
Would you like to see?

Look I know this text is garbage,
I also don't like Joyce.
I don't pick the curriculum,
so we don't have any choice.

Yes I know you'd like my subject more,
if we did more modern art.
Too bad, so sad that all our texts
are picked by dusty farts.

You don't want to be here
on a Friday afternoon?
Dude, neither.
I know that as a teacher
I just kinda live in the walls here
I'd really like to get to that.
Alas, we're stuck for now.

Oooh hell yeah!
We're learning about (X)!
Did you know I love (X)?
(X) is the whole reason
I even took this job!
Wait, what do you mean,
"(X) is old and boring"?
It only came out-
21 years ago.
Yeesh, thanks for that.

How is it that there's always one
who watches Ben Shapiro,
who thinks he'll set the femoids straight,
and be a local hero?
I've heard this same shit every year,
I wish you'd disappearo.
Like, maybe we're all triggered, but
You're gonna get a zero.

Hey bud.
I know they're nasty now.
I know it's hard to get past it.
But if you hit the other side,
the spark you have
is gonna light up lives.
You just have to keep it lit.
I can say it, because I was there too.

When I was still at Teacher School
the lecturer would often stress,
that when a student "gets it now",
that feeling is the very best.
And I though 'sure, it's probably nice,
but how good can it really be?'

But I was wrong, there's nothing quite
like knowing that you've learned from me.

I really can not stress enough,
I'll tell you what you need:
You'll always find your English rough
if you don't friggin' read!

Sometimes I think
"How did I deserve this?"
And then I remember
what I was like as a student,
And then I think
"Oh yeah".

Our kids get labelled harshly.
Too harshly, I would say.
the job can suck, but sometimes,
the kids will light the day.

Basic -OR- Sometimes Things are Popular Because They're Good

It's fine and well to want to criticise,
In fact I really do believe you should.
And beauty lives in the beholder's eyes,
but sometimes things are really just that good.

There was a show that came around
In Twenty-Zero-Five,
It bent its way out of the screen,
the world was so alive.
A charming lad and his two friends,
with magic martial arts,
The Boy Inside the Iceberg blew
his way into our hearts.

The gorgeous animation shone,
it had a stellar cast,
with fully realised characters
and challenges to pass.

The characters developed well,
and came into their own,
with unity and friendship, fell
a tyrant from the throne.

And sure maybe on paper,
it sounds okay at best,
it comes across as basic,
but put that thought to rest.
Go slightly deeper in, you'll find
A lot more there to love.
A show with all the elements
to rank it up above.

Not falling for the loud and overhyped
suggests that you can be a clever thinker,
but hating something just because it's liked?
Some thoughts are bad, but that's a massive
stinker.

The next one crawled onto the page
In Nineteen-Sixty-Two,
to change the world for kids like me,
bedecked in red and blue.
For once a teenaged sidekick who
stood out all on his own.
A bug who swung around the skies
instead of having flown.

And God, the text was cheesy as
he fought against a zoo
of Rhinos, Goblins, Octopi
and birds, to name a few.
He dealt with human problems, though
which made him feel more true;
It's hard to be a hero when
your rent is coming due.

Again, it's pretty basic
and not-at-all adult.
If you can't get behind it,
it can't be called a fault.
But simple things can so inspire
the strength when times are rough.
To stand against life's villains is
in simple terms, enough.

Your judgement should be deeper, go beyond;
the surface of a story's just the start.
The part of it that stays and lingers on
is all about the feelings it imparts.

The last one takes us back in time,
to Nineteen-Seven-Seven;
A juggernaut of silver screen,
the zenith of nerd-heaven.
It shapes the screen for forty years,
with such a gripping power.

A science fiction homage to
Akira Kurosawa.

A chosen one who walks the sky,
his little robot friends,
go off to save a princess 'fore
she meets a deadly end.
They stand against the Empire
and win the day of course,
by blowing up the deadly moon
with just a bit of Force.

We didn't even know back then,
He was the villain's son.
which told us that a hero could
be found in everyone.
And never underestimate
how much that message means,
when people in the Dark might need
some light upon their screens.

Okay, by now you've got it figured out;
I don't have all that much too deep to say.
I just wanted some time to talk about
some fiction that I really like today.

2018 Miles -OR- Miles, 2019

You came into our lives a gift for her,
and seeing you, it set her eyes alight.
The thing that at the time I couldn't know:
that having you would make it all so right.

I also couldn't comprehend the pain
from looking at your photographs tonight.

Twenty-Three/Oh-Three/Twenty-Eighteen

I'd had the plan to bring you home
At least far back as Christmas time.
And since that week she'd gone for work,
the timing had turned out sublime.

I'd bought the cage a while back,
and hid it safely at my Pop's,
So on her day of coming home,
I'd buy you from the shop.

When you were safe inside the car,
all tucked inside a box to go,
it struck me just how small you were,
my car had never gone so slow.

You Spider-Manned around the cage,
so that was how you got your name.
You couldn't be a Peter though,
Thank goodness Miles was fair game.

I watched all day, and she came home,
We loved you from that moment on,
and in my heart, you filled a hole
I never even knew was gone.

Twenty-Nine/Oh-Three/Twenty-Eighteen

You'd made yourself a fixture now.
It wasn't even one week past.
But you'd decided we were friends,
a love that had developed fast.

A painter's first time finding colour,
a baby learning how to see,
A child's first time tasting sugar;
compare with how you came to me.

I didn't know, 'til I knew you,
I'd love an animal as much.
And I don't think that you could know
how much impact was in your touch.

There's just one first, and you would be
the only first I'd ever get.
I can't believe how blessed I was
for you to be my first-time pet.

Fifteen/Oh-Five/Twenty-Eighteen

You've grown a bit, but even so,
the gamepad's twice as big as you.
But it's unfair that I can play;
you press on the controller too.

Eighteen/Oh-Five/Twenty-Eighteen

I'm going on a trip today,
to Brisbane I will soon be flown.
You've jumped into my bags to say
I'm not allowed to go alone.

Oh-Five/Oh-Seven/Twenty-Eighteen

The house has changed! It's different now!
The living space is so much more!
So this is where we learn how much
you love permission to explore

Twenty/Oh-One/Twenty-Nineteen

We've had a scare, you've had a fall,
your tum'll end up very sore,
and even though you've made it through,
I've never been so scared before.

Fourteen/Oh-Two/Twenty-Nineteen

You've been inside my heart a while,
you've grown to such a gorgeous rat.
You're cuddly and adorable,
and just the cutest kind of fat.

Eighteen/Ten/Twenty-Nineteen

The photos show the love you have,
your constant curiosity.
How cruel it is, the joy you have
was not for perpetuity.

Thirty-One/Twelve/Twenty-Nineteen

The person I am now did not exist,
before I'd seen your face, your fur, your paws.
So what we had was like a new lifetime,
and well, I guess for you, it really was.

I wish that you'd had better than you got.
I thought at least we'd have a few more years.
But on that Summer's day I found you there,
and learned my own capacity for tears.

You opened up a whole new part of me
the love you had was such a special kind.
It's one I never thought that I would have,
it's one that felt so wonderful to find.

I couldn't know, 'til you were in my life
I'd ever mourn an animal as much.
You weren't the last, and other rats have come,
but you alone could have your kind of touch.

There'll only ever get to be one first,
the most impactful first I'll ever get.
I can't describe the kind of pain you feel
when first you say goodbye to such a pet.

Now

I miss you Miles, all the time,
you loving, funny, cheeky lad.
Your memory stays with us though
in all the other rats we've had.
I'll never have another first,
but really that's not quite so bad.

Our memories are precious, Miles
I loved to be your ratty dad.

Not Ready -OR- Somehow a Very Surprising/Unsurprising Thing to Realise

Some things are inevitable.
The apple has to fall,
the river can't flow up,
The sun must mercifully set.
Time is endless, until it's not.

When he was eaten from within,
when he spend his life not living,
when he'd lost everything but time,
I was ready.
A decade of it for me,
I think, an eternity for him.
So even long before his time,
I was ready.
We'd known for years,

our peace was made for most of it.
So when he finally lost his time,
I was ready.

You've given me so much, been there for me.
You're the experience from which I've learned.
When I look up, you're part of what I see.
It scares me when I see how time has turned.
For you, I'm not ready.

When bonds became undone,
when glue became unstuck,
although it took a lot less time,
I was ready.
The cohesion of the unit meant more,
The cohesion that had already collapsed.
So knowing it was borrowed time,
I was ready.
It could have been more painful.
In an ideal world, maybe.
But in the moment, at the time,
I was ready.

In all that time, I've gained on you in age
but somehow you have always stayed ahead.
I'm wishing now you wouldn't turn the page,
or maybe even roll it back instead.
For you, I'm not ready.

Time's endless up until it isn't,
I think I've got a grasp on that.
So though I still have loads of time,
I hope I'll be ready.
My star's still so full of gas
(I'm frequently told you can smell it)
but even stars burn out in time.
I hope I'll be ready.
The Spectre's on my mind a lot,
an idea I've turned 'round a bit.
I'm trusting when I've had my time,
I hope I'll be ready.

We're older now, and though you seem less wise,
although I can't conceive you've more to tell,
the time we have is still a thing to prize,
and I know what it means to you as well.
For you, I'm not ready.

For you, I'm not ready.

The End -OR- This Book Can End, But I Won't Stop

I do enjoy a good beginning.
A middle part, those are fun.
But if you asked my favourite part,
I'd say "the ending one".

The journey's really cool and all,
but destinations are my jam.
You get to see how things have come
for people from where they began.

I really like the story's end,
perhaps a bit more than I should
I know Empire's the stronger film,
but I think Jedi's just as good.

The plots are all concluded, and
the characters can all go home,
The audience can leave as well
and think about how much they've grown.

The ending of a story arc,
(as long as it's done semi-well),
will leave me feeling warm inside
without a single gripe to tell.

I think my favourite thing about
a story coming to a close,
is how it never works like that,
it isn't how a real life goes.

There's never any falling out.
The characters go home fulfilled.
We never see the morning when
the Emperor's been up and killed.

And even now, in reboot world,
We only see them decades on,
in time to have another start,
and move another plot along.

But living doesn't go that way.
It's more than just the biggest scenes.
the normal people live their lives
inside the moments in-between.

The big events still happen though,
the things we all look forward to.
But in between the big events
we've all got lives and stuff to do.

A film gets to a wedding, and
it has a lovely, happy end.
When I get to my wedding, I
expect another day again.

We really don't get endings here,
that's kinda not what life's about.
The leaden blimp can come to roost,
then once again it must go out.

The big events can change us all,
but after that the book won't close.
Instead another chapter starts,
and we keep seeing how it goes.

The only time we really end
is at the point we end for real.
But even when you're in the ground
the ones you leave behind will heal.

Because we only get one end
I think that makes it matter more.
The time we spend between the scenes
is what those bigger scenes are for.

So that's why endings are so cool:
Because they're not realistic things.
They show us possibilities

that normal lives can never bring.

And then with life contrasted so,
it helps us to appreciate
the chances that we get to grow,
the chance to make the moments great.

We work towards the final page,
to put a big event to rest.
But then another chapter starts,
and who knows? It could be the best.

22/23 -OR- It's Nice to Think About How Stars Align Sometimes

When I met you, and you met me
at twenty-two and twenty-three
we changed each other's lives a lot,
but what if you and I had not?
What if inside another world
a different timeline had unfurled?

When I met you, at twenty-two,
you wanted to expand your range.
I think you wanted something new,
and saw in me a bit of change.

When you met me, at twenty-three,
I'd been all flipped around, about.
I needed some stability,
some help to sort the future out.

We met at such a perfect time
for each to help the other grow;
became each other's matching rhyme
became the people we now know.

At Twenty-Two and Twenty-Three,
when you and I became a 'we'.

If you met me at age thirteen,
would things have been the same?
I really doubt they would've been,
At thirteen I was super lame.

If you were twelve when first we met,
I think you would have hated me.
I had a lot of growing yet;
of learning basic empathy.

I'd hate for you to meet at twelve,
that stupid, undeveloped kid.
Forever wrapped inside himself,
before the growing that he did.

If you were twelve and I thirteen,
the life we have would not have been.

At thirty-three and thirty-two?
What if we'd met a decade late?
Would I be me, and you be you,
if that instead had been our fate?

Would we still meet each other then?
If we grew older separately?
It's hard to guess what happens when
I don't know you, nor you know me.

Perhaps we'd both grow better, or
perhaps instead we'd both be worse?
The only thing I'd say for sure,
our song would have a different verse.

I'd only hope we'd be a 'we'
at thirty-two and thirty-three.

A decade young, a decade late,
it's strange to think, to speculate.
But as for true reality,
I think we timed it perfectly.
No other day, no different night,
we met. It was exactly right.